About to Be Young

MONROE LAWRENCE

You

About to Be ng

THE ELEPHANTS

20 21 22 23 24 5 4 3 2 1

Distributed by Small Press Distribution, Inc.

The Elephants Ltd.
www.theelephants.net

ISBN 978-1-988979-42-7 print

Cover image by Anna Bonesteel

Book design by Aimee C. Harrison
Typeset in Garamond Premier Pro

Edited by Broc Rossell

hannah it is all done before it happens

—HANNAH WEINER

The head of God laid in my arms

—JOHN WIENERS

Hoops of miracle are peeling   from me as I advance
(don't look away(

they are peeling

Oh   they are peeling at high speed
th(e piston glows fuck-orange(

the dream is flowing over you

The dream is flowing   over you like beads

Driving up the hill

in the dream There is a line of

remonstrance Cars backed down the hill

They gleaming good shame

at my gift, at my folded

& final window, like glancing

Monroe! collect self! Pour language

the totaled car

Oh I love my mom

And dad so much upon waking:

& my best friend Lee upon waking

How
eloquent   the amethyst Testimony

Oh god
make me a beautiful poet

crying almond, almond, almond into the night

A wish to die, forever
        like Orpheus

Flaking the truth of my
young mouth.

What are the things I—

Nothing, not
family or romantic friends, only

The golden hold of poetry

Golden like a fad
of caring. A bowl of pottery.

with   Enormous

Fear   Iam the,
metal to the
Pistol;   And I

am The great,
love   of my own Life

I want to play seriously on the roof
with an enormous aptitude
for beads: peeling bad
          capital from myself,
          yet not despairing over the belief-
system taping the war to the sky.
Already it is fairly
          molten in its blue flaw.
          Wringing wet sleet
          from the stone connotes
          finally the tactic,
          of the belief-
          system: like
          the smooth grind of a sentence—
& our blinking concerns the beauty
of a hexagon sky. The night dots lift now:
on quilted tents with trees approaching: & to
          imagine it,
          with devastating
          pathos, we unfurl
          like a revolting battery.
The attacks can wait; nothing changes
their true power. And
          it *is* true,
          chanting this
          token
          fluency to the night
finally in memory of us, As if the
light soup pours / Off the flat of the knife

I cannot fit   inexpressiveness
Snowing my mouth

To picture that variety as intrinsic   Slurring up & down
            the object like   Marquetry .

     like the deer, Carcass   That   slid in a   meters
down the path.   that took six months.   Do I call that—say—
"with tectonic slowness"?   Leaving in its
wake a slug?   Like a wake? But that's not right.
Nothing would be, really

&With the jackhammer going,
&flakes of teal splitting off the acrylic shell,

A blur of mice surged unexpectedly from the opening.

                                                &literally on the other side, it
was the same thing with
bees. Except   they "poured forth upon the cruelty of the
          jackhammer."
A golden ointment to its blowing noise

I grinned through the entire
focused on death
Like him
my father another with swords

We were on some
holiday so I went,
fucking in the *hissing storm* down
Through the alien corn & a
Plausible gradient of thaw, chewing the
night sap like an embryonic
apple cuff was
splintering noir introduction;
it was not my intention to "splinter noir introduction"
so we
ate the curved risk of
"betting on the splinters by day" and
Right down through the baton &
Salience thorn this esoteric glabrous saliva made the
Lake ask suddenly of
Night such violet jagged shame it blew harm strings to the day

I agree. grace is the dribbling blindness

on
blue   glamor

tactical smoky limousine

how Ia ppear to
others. Of a slight unique –
They
shame themselves by
using it.
The fundamental
embarrass Of alive

Debased,

by Making literally,
any
Moves in the   world

Please, I felt broken
away,
Resisting to write out
in the other room

I could
held my book at my side, leaned
Back
and cried

the curled elegance   of a receipt

On wet
Speed in the library, the social
situations slide   Like beautiful wipers

until I am crying like a twinkling
diagram,
As if the whole

city were one,
grinding cocaine hierarchy.

And it must be my destiny:
fluent

in
Unassailable strings of braided syrup, to say

Obviously, there is a bold, shitty
Kind of

magic   to life .

I am thinking,
Only

of my enemies tonight

in the dark caves where they are
And living as if they, enjoyed me
somehow

In the cold doldrums   of their world.

Surely   they are making their moves upon the world
With great strident steps toward   "a teeming   Desiderata."

I know
they are wielding the mutant   flaming

trident
outward in long flaring sweeps

against this darkness   Which threatens to consume them
          also.

My potent enemies.
Navigating the world like a glinting sperm.

this poem is to my enemies

I feel toward them:

as to the hulking   Dragoon bullies of old

subject to
desire—
a quite purple & forlorn desire

A dozen in another rage
In failing to limp now
To set fire the ruin plant
To come with us in failing

the land escapes around you

Anyway the land escapes around you

Tonight I apply, the numb cream in chords.
it is quite

Beautiful vaseline emotion

There is a dark, crowbar of paranoia
Passive

against
the drilled   sky of my arms

Bleeding   traditional stillness. And it is

In my breast to react.
And it is the same sorry beep of a trap.
And it is in

the mind of the line, such
predilection for the lucent artery
Brilliant

with dark comprehension to

Bear me, with extraordinary
disgust for it, so I sleep as the slender Tool

the throat
lumps,   When we are born
The doves of   love,
have   Happened

the   Frame was traced against the wall   &removed. Outside t
Was snowing. Outside

                    snowing. Traced decision, Snot-wet.Push   you in a Lie
to the wall. I had   fantasize about, my

Body   thrives in glass

The wilderness

For the sake of slovenly human
leisure; that is the tongue rolling
Behind the cheeks, a glazed Breeze i would
only.
later realize

Honest to God I can't. Fluttering with micro-lie. I am a .
I am Eating cake. I am eating pang cakes. I am eating
pang . I walk out in the snow. You had your Moment
I had mine. I wanted
" Experience
wind -shield. you asked,
what does the factory Make? Factories
Across
& A rash of lamb belts
& I walk out in the snow. I make in the Ha. (still I
experience itas a lack.) Still experience Lack. I
walk into the snow. I experience it as a
Lack. everything Relates. the axe slams
Kindness into the tree

Mom I am   .   this not   As it,   sounds. I am   Boy
          & it is snowing. the flaps
on the   Wing
tweeze
Upward   & then down.   Mom we have begun our descent

Pure shy. I walk out in the snow
I walk out in the snow. Pixels flake. apart like crumbled . I
am moving
through
Solid flood. I am moving through The blush,
tin burst of pan

“nephew-genital”   is the worst Word: it   berates upon niece
like Anything: a most Berserk   intaglio of dice

the animal
inside my father
does not tremble
I know but can

The gregarious legends are gone now in the red showers
Nothing but golden sentiment from now on
And other esoteric shelter greebled across the night

I’ve moved, like clasped
hands Into a mullet
dog   from Behind, the last
mirror   Is on earth

too panted
sordid blowing elephans
swell the hot lane
feling bitter
with spat of
want malaise
gravy anger held
aloft these elephans dipe now
into sponged supply
to menace peace
one second time
with circumspection these produce
their dripping breath
extente that monie
elephans followt me
home
a darken tactic
with specious time on earth
I give her that
to of couse be-neath
the arns rod
my god saw god

High in the saddle
In the grass of my problemms again
In overlapping maile armor
And peering formational ennemi   sans problem
To conquer as these knights prolept
Your mounted honour
And the troop felt   relevant engorged
By muscle tonight in cold victorie

I
edit
the violets myself

To
speak of it

as a   Fraying secret

Boy starving into me
the
entrance
bones   Her beautiful head

Being   seen isn't quite like that

Like can't anna
herself   unsure
The task off

falls from the quilt
like can't Anna
In   damage to eat listening

Comb   lies across
falls from the quilt

then he stood quickly without guilt
herself unsure
High heels in the snow

So
long   in the shadow of our intimacy

to Blue out the ending

Of a colour you were wearing
approaching my front arms

There is a moment, I want
again, I
would like to unwatch
when
it seems
you take your glasses off, again
between us,
and I cannot be harmed
through two windows, rather bald, and
And again, you folding shirts
by the dark
sky
to wipe
The daydream
I would have
yes? to
keep it

Pouring   your shoulders off
the roaring pond

There is no saint for this

to eat
Truly from   your mercy

Even
in the sympathy
embraced – the humid – the sugar
of distance, & prescribed
distraction summer, aloft, even
overwhelmed with goodness
& human alarm
for one another – a folded
harm I
know – the irksome & psychic
dent, I – it – I
can still be penetrated
by
smell by
memory of you & by spring

well How did you expect   that to deplete

well How did you expect the tableau to deplete? I re-
walked the whole thing.   you had   thrown me something, i
remarked on that a Year ago,   almost a difficult—shelf-like
buildings.   quoted some idiot, &before i even finished I
learned the power of your reward: it was just, certain muscles
of the face. but I have. not   seen this town. How? how not.
where squares of sheer colour are the sky

Growing   rain upon my face

alive between dawn
climbs to tension
Anna in a field of larks

(oh god.
Lights off Anna

In my mind I
hard a-

gainst my face
like
Washing my face

I’m not

one of Those
carers

am I

At the table I felt, for a time
it seemed
the world was human colours
The long
room
of thinking filled
with furniture, of your family,
A dynamic slowly
seething
in the air behind
my conception of,
you & the long grains
of detail
piling
Into
half-understanding

a lullaby above heaven
In the car with mother
Beside two other cars

My mother hugs me
after I
have been called, I
have
been away
She would cry on,
holding Up
the damp light,—my
conflict
writhes apart.
She
puts her
hand
in the lease
of only family tonight—
Where the
weapon is,
A velvet daughter

coils of
spreading truant steam
darkens as something to know
morning coast

as if gloat offer they
shows through so
are you
and is it

even there
such smart as brow muscle
releases safe
such cached like

wind turning down the field
the riot quiets
down
to reach new

distance
as if talking me
by sheer lamé
as if knowing both

Moral girls
Had a road trip.
been
kind to me.
We
, Oh
god I think, To rob us of
memory
Once & for all.
& I think
a love can
Ache
right through you.
the front, seat
There is a
panic dialectic. I stepped
Into it

In Greece, the pastel
boxes
clicked.
Alien Belgians
in a
white sheet—
beautiful.
Screaming to the wind & cicada.
& Nothing
could
break Me,
for the
intermittent
burst
of sky   And sky

Walking into the low   clearing of the leasing
dawn,
I can   read by that

your cone of   reasons maybe.
Well, maybe.
&suddenly it   comes to me,

pushing your hair back like
steam, & I
See that mindfulness glowing   out from you, oh profane

longing, &
oh maybe nothing can touch me,
make any

other thing
matter again, On into the
night or the light honestly whichever

The legend skis up alongside
In soft humility
it has always been this way

the evening they take

sky to the police
given up lips to become thin
again though you were always good

to find out
pushing fine fire
has a small
mood

oh porch
the low & buzzing granite
crouching rain
a bowl of weather

the tract   of startled
molten dark ran down like gods paint roller
you see from the highway
and did   men-images
climb

            in descending
rappel of me
As now as unknown
on spokes of lavender foam

I told my gran an eye trick
She told me how to do
She told me since I told her that
A trick she longer knew

Tonight if you could drive
your car, by
dream
The interior light on, so I could recognize
So you recognize me
& stop
Like a narrative so
perfect, it floats
up and
down the night
And within it, to offer
the paper-bag colour iced coffee
Tonight is wet air, wet
clothing
and somehow
That
would make it
really last

Acknowledgments

Thanks to Cole Swensen for reading my poems. Thank you Broc Rossell, Moníca de la Torre, Vi Khi Nao, Jenny Penberthy, Rebekah Rutkoff, Peter Quartermain, and Andrea Actis. Thanks to Felix Bernstein for the support and the almonds into the night. Forrest Gander and CD Wright, thank you. Thank you Jessica Baer, Emma Wipperman, and Louise Akers. Thanks Ada Smailbegović. Thank you to Katie Foster for the repeated sky. Love and thanks to Alex Toy, Cary Stough, Carolyn Bergonzo, Krishan Mistry, Patricio Ferrari, and Patrick Riedy. Love to Lee Cannon-Brown, Anna Bonesteel, Torben Robertson, Forrest Elliott, and Cameron Parro. Thanks, finally, to my parents for singing and reading to me and for taking such care of me.

Bio

MONROE LAWRENCE was born on Vancouver Island, Canada. His childhood and most of his life were spent on ancestral Coast Salish, Musqueam, Squamish, and Tsleil-Waututh territories. He currently lives in Rhode Island on ancestral Narragansett and Wampanoag lands. *About to Be Young* is his first book.

Oh I love my mom
And dad so much upon waking:
& my best friend Lee   upon waking